Tucholsky Wagner Zola Scott Sydow Fonatne Freud Schlegel
Turgenev Wallace
Twain Walther von der Vogelweide Fouqué Friedrich II. von Preußen
Weber Freiligrath Frey
Kant Ernst
Fechner Fichte Weiße Rose von Fallersleben Richthofen Frommel
Hölderlin
Engels Fielding Eichendorff Tacitus Dumas
Fehrs Faber Flaubert
Eliasberg Ebner Eschenbach
Feuerbach Maximilian I. von Habsburg Fock Zweig Eliot
Ewald Vergil
Goethe London
Elisabeth von Österreich
Mendelssohn Balzac Shakespeare Dostojewski Ganghofer
Lichtenberg Rathenau Doyle Gjellerup
Trackl Stevenson Hambruch
Mommsen Tolstoi Lenz Droste-Hülshoff
Thoma Hanrieder
von Arnim Hägele Hauff Humboldt
Dach Verne
Reuter Rousseau Hagen Hauptmann Gautier
Karrillon Garschin
Defoe Baudelaire
Damaschke Hebbel
Descartes Hegel Kussmaul Herder
Wolfram von Eschenbach Dickens Schopenhauer
Darwin Melville Grimm Jerome Rilke George
Bronner Bebel Proust
Campe Horváth Aristoteles Voltaire Federer
Bismarck Vigny Barlach Herodot
Gengenbach Heine
Storm Casanova Tersteegen Grillparzer Georgy
Chamberlain Lessing Langbein Gilm Gryphius
Brentano Lafontaine
Strachwitz Claudius Schiller Kralik Iffland Sokrates
Schilling
Katharina II. von Rußland Bellamy Raabe Gibbon Tschechow
Gerstäcker
Löns Hesse Hoffmann Gogol Wilde Gleim Vulpius
Luther Heym Hofmannsthal Morgenstern
Roth Klee Hölty Goedicke
Heyse Klopstock Kleist
Luxemburg Homer Mörike
Puschkin Musil
Machiavelli La Roche Horaz
Kierkegaard Kraft Kraus
Navarra Aurel Musset
Nestroy Marie de France Lamprecht Kind Kirchhoff Hugo Moltke
Laotse Ipsen Liebknecht
Nietzsche Nansen Ringelnatz
Marx
von Ossietzky Lassalle Gorki Klett Leibniz
May vom Stein Lawrence Irving
Petalozzi Knigge
Platon Pückler Michelangelo Kafka
Sachs Poe Kock
Liebermann
de Sade Praetorius Mistral Zetkin Korolenko

Division of Words Rules for the Division of Words at the Ends of Lines, with Remarks on Spelling, Syllabication and Pronunciation

Frederick W. (Frederick William) Hamilton

Imprint

This book is part of the TREDITION CLASSICS series.

Author: Frederick W. (Frederick William) Hamilton
Cover design: toepferschumann, Berlin (Germany)

Publisher: tredition GmbH, Hamburg (Germany)
ISBN: 978-3-8491-8461-2

www.tredition.com
www.tredition.de

PREFACE

The principal purpose of this book is to give in brief form the rules and usages governing the division of words when the measure will not permit ending the word and the line together. This matter is considered in its relation to good spacing and to the legibility of the printed page.

Leading up to the discussion will be found some consideration of spelling, the formation of syllables, pronunciation, and accent. This consideration is necessarily brief, and no attempt has been made to give the rules for spelling which are so frequently found in spelling books, or any of them. In the writer's opinion such rules are of very little practical value. Good spelling is not so much the result of remembering and applying rules as it is of observation, practice, and memory. The lists of certain types of troublesome words may be found useful for ready reference.

Syllable formation, pronunciation, and accent are considered because it is hoped that the volumes of this series, particularly those in Part VI (Correct Literary Composition) and Part VIII (History of Printing), will contribute something to the general education of the apprentice as well as to his skill in the trade.

CONTENTS

DIVISION OF WORDS

The division of words when the words do not exactly fit the register of the line has always been a source of trouble. In the days of the manuscript makers devices such as crowding letters, reducing their size, or omitting them altogether were freely used and words were arbitrarily divided when the scribes so desired. During the greater part of the time every scribe divided as he pleased, often in ways which seem very strange to us, like the Greek custom of dividing always after a vowel and even dividing words of one syllable. With the invention of printing, however, the number of these devices was greatly diminished. It became a matter of spacing out the line or dividing the word. Of course that meant frequent word division and called for a systematization of rules with regard to this division. These rules for division are necessarily based on spelling and syllabication.

SPELLING

The idea that there is one right way to combine the letters representing a certain sound or group of sounds, that is a word, and that all other ways are wrong and little short of shameful is a comparatively new idea among us. The English speaking folk held down to a comparatively recent time that any group of letters which approximately represented the sound was amply sufficient as a symbol of the word. This sort of phonetic spelling was commonly followed, and followed with great freedom. No obligation was recognized to be consistent. In ordinary writing, such as letters and the like, it is not unusual to find the same word spelled in a variety of ways in the same document.

[2] The last century has brought about an attempt to standardize spelling into conventional forms any departure from which is regarded as highly derogatory to the writer. In many cases these forms are fixed arbitrarily, and in some there is even now disagreement among the highest authorities. These difficulties and disagreements have two reasons: First, English is a composite language, drawn from many sources and at many periods; hence purely philological and etymological influences intervene, sometimes with marked results, while there is a difference of opinion as to how far these influences ought to prevail. Second, the English language uses an alphabet which fits it very badly. Many letters have to do duty for the expression of several sounds, and sometimes several of them have nearly or quite the same sound. For example, there are a number of distinct sounds of *a*, *i*, and *o* while *g* is sometimes indistinguishable from *j* and *c* from *k*. This is not always a matter of modification of sounds by the sounds of other letters combined with them. One has to learn how to pronounce *cough*, *dough*, *enough*, and *plough*, the *ough* having four distinct sounds in these four words. Each one of these sounds, by the way, could be exactly as well represented by another combination of letters which would be unmistakable, viz., *coff*, *doe*, *enuff*, and *plow*. It is impossible to tell except by the context either the pronunciation or the meaning of *bow*. If the *ow* is pronounced as in *low*, it means a weapon. If the *ow* is pronounced as in *cow* it may mean either an obeisance or the front end of a boat.

This standardization of spelling is unfortunately not quite complete, although nearly so. Concerning the vast majority of the words in the English language there is no difference of opinion. A few words are differently spelled by different authorities. There are seven of these authorities of the first rank, three English, Stormonth, the Imperial Dictionary, and the Oxford Dictionary; and four American, Webster's International, Worcester, the Century Dictionary, and the Standard Dictionary. American printers may ordinarily disregard the English authorities.

[3] Any one of the four American authorities may be safely followed. In cases where two spellings are given in the dictionary consulted, take the first one. Ordinarily a printing office adopts one of the great authorities as a standard and conforms the office style to it. All office copy will follow it and all errors in copy from outside will be corrected by it. Spellings differing from it will be regarded as errors, even though supported by other authorities.

This rule, however, is subject to one very important exception. The author has an unquestionable right to choose his own dictionary or to use any spelling for which there is any authority, English or American. If he has his own ideas on the subject of spelling he should be very careful that his manuscript is correctly spelled according to his ideas, and clearly written or typed. He should also indicate on the manuscript the authority he wishes used in correcting the spelling in case of mistakes or illegible passages. Every care should be taken to make the manuscript copy as correct as possible and as legible as possible. Such care may be very troublesome at first, but it will result in great saving of expense.

In addition to the authorities named there are the rules and "reformed" spellings adopted by the American Philological Association and published by the United States Government. These are followed fully in some offices, partly in others, and in many not at all. This is a question of the office style and the author's wish. If copy is clear and spelled according to any authority, it is the compositor's duty to follow it. If it is misspelled or illegible he is to correct it according to the office style unless otherwise directed by the author in writing. If furnished with such a direction he is to follow it. This procedure will clear the compositor of all blame. Any questions which then arise lie between the author and the proofreader.

In the case of the reformed spellings, however, the departure from the ordinary appearance of the words is so great that the author cannot be allowed full freedom to set aside the office style. If he is paying for the printing he may insist on his spelling. If he is contributing to a [4] periodical and the printing is done at the publisher's expense it is for the publisher to determine the style of printing to be used.

Any full consideration of the question of reformed spelling is hardly in place in this book. The author may perhaps be permitted one observation. Innovation in the use of the English language would appear to be primarily the work of scholars, and the adoption of such innovations would seem to belong to the book printer rather than to the commercial printer. The public mind as a whole is conservative. It is not hospitable to changes and does not soon become aware of them, much less familiar with them. The commercial printer makes his appeal to the mind of the general public. He will do well to use a vehicle familiar, intelligible, and acceptable to it.

Correct spelling is mainly a matter of habit and observation. To a certain extent it is a matter of careful pronunciation, but this is not always a safe or even a possible guide. The vowels preceding or following the one on which the primary accent falls, sometimes called obscure vowels, are so slurringly pronounced that even a pedantic precision will hardly make it possible to indicate clearly which vowel is used. The writer remembers seeing an examination paper written by a fourth year medical student in which the word *fever* was spelled *fevor*. A moment's thought will show that so far as pronunciation is concerned the word might be spelled *fevar*, *fevir*, *fevor*, *fever*, or *fevur* without any appreciable difference. The correct spelling is merely a matter of observation.

The author has on his desk at the moment of writing these lines half a dozen good books, each containing a set of rules for spelling. From these it would be easy to compile a set of fairly good rules. Each of these rules, however, has exceptions, in some cases quite numerous. To remember these rules with their exceptions would be a considerable mental task and to apply them would be cumbrous and time consuming. The effort would probably resolve itself into an actual learning of the words which present difficulties. The best way to become a good [5] speller is to form the habit of careful reading, observing the form of every word as it passes before the eye and so unconsciously fixing it in the memory. The dictionary should be consulted whenever there is any doubt.

If you are to write a word, call up a mental picture of it, and if the picture is not perfectly clear go to the dictionary and fix a correct image of it in your mind. Be careful to pronounce every word you use as correctly as possible and you will get all the aid pronunciation can give you. Careless speaking and careless reading are the two great sources of incorrect spelling.

The following tables will be found useful in settling practice with regard to certain troublesome classes of words.

American usage tends to the termination *-ize* where English usage often sanctions *-ise*. Use the termination *-ise* in

advertise
advise
appraise
apprise (*to inform*)
arise
chastise
circumcise
comprise
compromise
demise
devise
disfranchise
disguise
emprise
enfranchise
enterprise
exercise
exorcise
franchise
improvise
incise
merchandise
premise
reprise
revise
rise
supervise
surmise
surprise

Use the termination *-ize* or *-yze* in

aggrandize
agonize

analyze
anatomize
anglicize
apologize
apostrophize
apprize (*to value*)
authorize
baptize
brutalize
canonize
catechize
catholicize
cauterize
centralize
characterize
christianize
civilize
colonize
criticize
crystallize
demoralize
dogmatize
economize
[6] emphasize
epitomize
equalize
eulogize
evangelize
extemporize
familiarize
fertilize
fossilize
fraternize
galvanize
generalize
gormandize
harmonize
immortalize
italicize

jeopardize
legalize
liberalize
localize
magnetize
memorialize
mesmerize
metamorphize
methodize
minimize
modernize
monopolize
moralize
nationalize
naturalize
neutralize
organize
ostracize
paralyze
particularize
pasteurize
patronize
philosophize
plagiarize
pulverize
realize
recognize
reorganize
revolutionize
satirize
scandalize
scrutinize
signalize
solemnize
soliloquize
specialize
spiritualize
standardize
stigmatize

subsidize
summarize
syllogize
symbolize
sympathize
tantalize
temporize
tranquilize
tyrannize
universalize
utilize
vaporize
vitalize
vocalize
vulcanize
vulgarize

II

Use the termination *-ible* in the following words:

accessible
admissible
appetible
apprehensible
audible
cessible
coercible
compatible
competible
comprehensible
compressible
conceptible
contemptible
contractible
controvertible
convertible
convincible
corrigible
corrosible
corruptible
credible
decoctible
deducible
defeasible
defensible
descendible
destructible
digestible
discernible
distensible
divisible
docible
edible
effectible
[7] eligible

eludible
enforcible
evincible
expansible
expressible
extendible
extensible
fallible
feasible
fencible
flexible
forcible
frangible
fusible
gullible
horrible
illegible
immiscible
impassible
intelligible
irascible
legible
miscible
negligible
partible
passible (*susceptible*)
perceptible
permissible
persuasible
pervertible
plausible
possible
producible
reducible
reflexible
refrangible
remissible
reprehensible
resistible

responsible
reversible
revertible
risible
seducible
sensible
tangible
terrible
transmissible
visible

In all other cases use *-able*.

III

The following nouns end in *-er*.

abetter
abstracter
accepter
adapter
adviser
affirmer
aider
almoner
annoyer
arbiter
assenter
asserter
bailer
caster
censer (vessel)
concocter
condenser
conferrer
conjurer
consulter
continuer
contradicter
contriver
convener
conveyer
corrupter
covenanter
debater
defender
deliberater
deserter
desolater
deviser
discontinuer
disturber

entreater
exalter
exasperater
exciter
executer (*except in law*)
expecter
frequenter
granter
idolater
imposer
impugner
incenser
inflicter
insulter
interceder
interpreter
interrupter
[8] inviter
jailer
lamenter
mortgager (*except in law*)
obliger
obstructer
obtruder
perfecter
perjurer
preventer
probationer
propeller
protester
recognizer
regrater
relater
respecter
sailer (*ship*)
sorcerer
suggester
supplanter
upholder

vender

The following nouns end in *-or*.

abbreviator
abductor
abettor (*law*)
abominator
abrogator
accelerator
acceptor
accommodator
accumulator
actor
adjudicator
adjutor
administrator
admonitor
adulator
adulterator
aggregator
aggressor
agitator
amalgamator
animator
annotator
antecessor
apparitor
appreciator
arbitrator
assassinator
assessor
benefactor
bettor
calculator
calumniator
captor
castor (*oil*)
censor

coadjutor
collector
competitor
compositor
conductor
confessor
conqueror
conservator
consignor
conspirator
constrictor
constructor
contaminator
contemplator
continuator
contractor
contributor
corrector
councillor
counsellor
covenantor (*law*)
creator
creditor
cultivator
cunctator
debtor
decorator
delator (*law*)
denominator
denunciator
depredator
depressor
deteriorator
detractor
dictator
dilator
director
dissector
disseizor

disseminator
distributor
divisor
dominator
donor
effector
elector
elevator
elucidator
emulator
enactor
[9] equivocator
escheator
estimator
exactor
excavator
exceptor
executor (*law*)
exhibitor
explorator
expositor
expostulator
extensor
extirpator
extractor
fabricator
factor
flexor
fornicator
fumigator
generator
gladiator
governor
grantor (*law*)
habitator
imitator
impostor
impropriator
inaugurator

inceptor
incisor
inheritor
initiator
innovator
insinuator
institutor
instructor
interlocutor
interpolator
interrogator
inventor
investor
juror
lector
legator
legislator
lessor
mediator
modulator
monitor
mortgagor (*law*)
multiplicator
narrator
navigator
negotiator
nonjuror
numerator
objector
obligor (*law*)
observator
operator
originator
pacificator
participator
peculator
percolator
perforator
perpetrator

persecutor
perturbator
possessor
preceptor
precursor
predecessor
predictor
prevaricator
procrastinator
procreator
procurator
professor
progenitor
projector
prolocutor
promulgator
propagator
propitiator
proprietor
prosecutor
protector
protractor
purveyor
recognizor (*law*)
recriminator
reflector
regenerator
regulator
relator (*law*)
rotator
sacrificator
sailor (*seaman*)
scrutator
sculptor
sectator
selector
senator
separator
sequestrator

servitor
solicitor
spectator
spoliator
sponsor
successor
suitor
supervisor
suppressor
surveyor
survivor
[10] testator
tormentor
traitor
transgressor
translator
valuator
vendor (*law*)
venerator
ventilator
vindicator
violator
visitor

IV

Words which in their shortest form end in *-d, -de, -ge, -unit, -rt, -se, -sr,* take the ending *-sion;* e.g., *abscind, abscission; include, inclusion; emerge, emersion; remit, remission; infuse, infusion; repress, repression.*

All others take the ending *-tion.*

The following are irregularities:

adhesion
assertion
attention
coercion
cohesion
crucifixion
declension
dimension
dissension
distortion
divulsion
expulsion
impulsion
insertion
intention
occasion
propulsion
recursion
repulsion
revulsion
scansion
suspicion
tension
version

Words ending in *-ance, -ence; -ancy, -ency; -ant,* and *-ent,* often cause confusion when carelessly written.

The following is a list of the more common words with the *e* form.

abducent
abhorrence, -ent
abluent
absent, -ence
absorbent
abstergent
abstinence, -ent
adherence, -ent
advertency, -ent
affluence, -ent
antecedence, -ent
apparent
appertinent
appetence, -ency
ardent
benevolence, -ent
circumference
coexistence
coherence, -ent
coincidence, -ent
competence, -ent
concurrence, -ent
condolence
[11] conference
confidence, -ent
confluence, -ent
consentient
consequence
consequent
consistence, -ent
consistency
constituent
continence, -ent
convenience, -ent
corpulence, -ent
correspondence, -ent
currency, -ent
deference
delinquency, -ent

dependence, -ent
deponent
descendent (*adj.*)
despondency, -ent
difference
diffidence, -ent
diffluent
efficiency, -ent
eminence, -ency
eminent
excellence, -ency
excellent
existence, -ent
expediency
feculence, -ent
flocculence, -ent
fluency, -ent
fraudulence, -ent
imminence, -ent
impatience, -ent
impellent
imprudence, -ent
impudence, -ent
incipience, -ent
incumbency, -ent
independence, -ent
indolence, -ent
inference
inherence, -ent
intermittent
iridescence, -ent
lambent
latency, -ent
leniency, -ent
magniloquence, -ent
malevolence, -ent
mellifluence, -ent
mollient
obedience, -ent

occurrence, -ent
omniscience, -ent
opulence, -ency
opulent
patience, -ent
pendent (*adj.*)
pendency
penitence, -ent
permanence, -ent
permanency
pertinence, -ent
pestilence, -ent
poculent
portent
potency, -ent
precedence, -ent
preference
prescience, -ent
presence, -ent
presidency, -ent
proficiency, -ent
prominence, -ent
proponent
[12] providence, -ent
prudence, -ent
purulence, -ent
quintessence
recurrence, -ent
reference
refluence, -ent
repellent
residence, -ency
resident
resolvent
resplendence, -ent
respondent
reverence, -ent
sentient
solvency, -ent

somnolency, -ent
subserviency, -ent
subsidence, -ency
subsistence, -ent
succulent
superintendence
superintendency
superintendent
tendence, -ency
transcendence, -ent
transcendency
transference
transient
transparency, -ent
transplendency, -ent
turbulence, -ent
vicegerency, -ent
virulence, -ent

Nearly all other words of this type take the *a* form.

The instructor should drill the pupils in spelling not only these "catch" words, but a wide range of English words. These lessons may be taken to advantage from some of the books mentioned in the list for supplementary reading, from any other good spelling book, or even from the pages of any well printed book or magazine. The words should be given out orally and written down by the pupil. A good exercise is the reading of a paragraph from any good book, or some stanza of poetry, the passage read to be taken down by the pupil with care to spell, punctuate, and capitalize properly.

A number of topics sometimes treated under the head of spelling will be found discussed in the "Printer's Manual of Style" (No. 41).

PRONUNCIATION

The English language is a difficult one to pronounce as well as to spell. This arises from two causes. The English language has some sounds not generally found in [13] other languages, such as *w* and *th*. As has already been pointed out, the alphabet fits the language very badly. Careful lexicographers indicate no less than seven sounds of *a*, five of *e*, three of *i*, four of *o* and six of *u*, as shown in the following table:

ā as in āle
[Ia] as in sen[Ia]te
ă as in ăm
á as in ásk
[a:] as in [a:]ll
ä as in fäther
(a) as in fin(a)l

ē as in ēve
ĕ as in ĕnd
[Ie] as in ev[Ie]nt
ẽ as in fẽrn
(e) as in prud(e)nce

ī as in īce
[Ii] as in [Ii]dea
ĭ as in pĭn

ō as in ōld
[Io] as in [Io]pen
ŏ as in ŏdd
ô as in ôrb

ū as in ūse
[Iu] as in [Iu]nite
ŭ as in ŭp
[u:] as in r[u:]de
[u=] as in f[u=]ll
û as in ûrn

In addition to these there are diphthongs, combinations of vowel sounds pronounced as one syllable, such as

ou as in *out*
oi as in *oil*

There are also a number of digraphs or combinations of vowels or consonants which have but one sound, such as

ai as in *rain*
eo as in *people*
ou as in *soup*
ou as in *soul*
ph as in *phalanx*
ch as in *chorus* or *chair*

C has two sounds, hard before *a, o,* and *u,* as in *cat, cot,* and *cut,* and soft before *e, i,* and *y,* as in *cell, city,* and *cycle.*

G has two sounds, hard before *a, o,* and *u,* as in *gate, gone,* and *gun,* soft before *e, i,* and *y,* as in *gem, gin,* and *gyve,* although it is sometimes hard before *i* as in *girl.*

Ch is sometimes soft as in *chair* and *arch,* and sometimes hard as in *choir.*

[14] *Th* has two sounds, soft, or surd, as in *thin* and *death,* and hard, or sonant, as in *then* and *smooth.*

S has two sounds, soft, or surd, as in *soft* and *this,* and hard, or sonant, as in *has* and *wise.*

We have, therefore, twenty-six letters with which to express fifty or more sounds, not counting the digraphs and diphthongs.

Correct pronunciation depends upon three things, correct sounding of the letters, correct division into syllables, and correct placing of the accent.

A syllable is the smallest separately articulated, or pronounced, element in speech, or one of the parts into which speech is broken. It consists of a vowel alone or accompanied by one or more consonants and separated by them, or by a pause, from a preceding or following vowel. This division of words into syllables is indicated in dictionaries by the use of the hyphen thus: *sub-trac-tion, co-or-din-ate.* It will be observed that in the first of these examples the vowels are all separated by consonants, while in the second two of them are separated by a pause only.

The English language has the further peculiarity of using *l* and *n* as vowels in syllabication, as in *middle* (*mid-dl*) and *reck-on* (*reck-n*).

The illustrations from this point to the end of this section on page 16 are not typographic divisions. They concern pronunciation only.

The division of words into syllables for pronunciation is generally, but not always, the same as that which should be followed in case the word has to be divided typographically. As these textbooks are intended to help the apprentice as a speaker and writer of English as well as a printer, it is worth while to give some attention to syllabication for pronunciation before proceeding to discuss typographical division.

Two letters forming a diphthong or digraph are not to be separated. *Coin-age* (*oi* diphthong) but *co-in-ci-dence* (*oi* not a diphthong). *Excess* (*ss* digraph, pronounced practically like a single s) gives *ex-cess-es, ex-cess-ive*, etc. Whether or not the letters thus occurring together form a diphthong or digraph will depend on the derivation of [15] the word, thus in *cat-head* (verb), a nautical term, *th* is not a digraph but in *ca-the-dral th* is a digraph, as is usually the case with these two letters. You would not say *cat-hed-ral*.

Two vowels, or a vowel and a diphthong, coming together but sounded separately belong to separate syllables.

A-or-ta, co-op-er-ate, but *coop-er-age, moi-e-ty.*

Do not end a syllable with

(*a*) *c* or *g* when soft, *en-ti-cing,* but *dic-tion, wa-ges* but *wag-on.*

(*b*) *t, s, z, c, sc, g,* and *d,* when followed by *i* or *e* giving the sound of *sh; ra-tion-al, o-cean, re-gion, as-cen-sion.*

(*c*) *d, s, t,* and *z* when followed by *u* giving the sound of *ch, sh, zh,* or *j, cen-sure, sei-zure, na-ture, ver-dure.*

Do not begin a syllable with

(*a*) *x* with the sound of *ks* or *gs, anx-ious, ex-act-ly.*

(*b*) *r* preceded by *a* or *e*; *par-ent, av-er-age,* but by exception, *pa-rent-al.*

(*c*) Single *l, n,* or *v,* followed by *i* with the sound of *y* consonant; *fol-io (fol-yo), gen-ius (gen-yus), sav-ior (sav-yor).*

Prefixes and suffixes are generally separated, *yel-low-ish, eat-able, pre-lude.* This last word is sometimes pronounced *prel-ude* and this pronunciation has some dictionary support, but it is objectionable.

A consonant or digraph between two sounded vowels usually joins the following vowel, *rea-son, no-ti-fy, mo-ther.*

When two or three consonants capable of beginning a syllable come between two sounded vowels they may all be joined to the following vowel.

(*a*) When the preceding vowel is long and accented; *en-a-bling, He-brew, i-dler.*

(*b*) When the following vowel is an accented syllable; *o-blige, re-dress.*

When two or three consonants capable of beginning a syllable come between two sounded vowels one may be joined to the pre-ceding vowel.

(*a*) When the vowel is short; *tab-let, res-cue, mus-ket.*

[16] (*b*) When the consonants are *st, str,* or *sp,* if either the preced-ing or following vowel is accented; *mis-tress, aus-tere, oys-ter, sus-pect.*

When a consonant is doubled (not forming a digraph) the two are generally separated; *beg-gar, bril-liant, cun-ning.*

The old-fashioned method of oral spelling by syllables *m-a-s-mas-t-e-r-ter-master* will be found extremely useful in teaching correct syllabication. It is recommended that constant use be made of it in spelling drill.

ACCENT

When a word consists of two syllables one of them receives more stress of voice than the other. This stress of voice is called accent. If the word consists of three or more syllables there is usually another syllable stressed in somewhat less degree. This is called a secondary accent. In some cases there may even be a third accent if the word is very long; *In'-come, val-e-tu'-di-na'-ri-an.* This fact arises from the tendency natural to all human speech to take more or less musical forms. The monotony of a series of stressed or of unstressed sounds would be unbearable. The pronunciation of such a series would be a highly artificial and very difficult performance. Correct pronunciation is very greatly concerned with the proper placing of the accent. Indeed the meaning of a familiar word may be quite obscured by a misplaced accent. For example, *he-red'-it-ary* is a very familiar word, but when pronounced *he-red-it'-ary,* as it was habitually by a friend of the author, we have to stop and think before catching the meaning.

The placing of the accent in English is subject to two general rules.

I The accent clings to the syllable which gives the meaning to the word, or in technical terms, the root syllable, *re-call', in-stall', in-stal-la'-tion* (accent falling on the syllable which defines the word as a noun), *in-her'-it.*

II Where the root syllable is not known the accent falls on the first syllable, with secondary accents following at intervals to relieve the voice.

[17] This last tendency not infrequently supersedes the other, partly from the natural habit of the language, and partly because the average man is not an etymologist and knows very little about the derivation of the words he uses. For example, in Shakespeare's time English people followed the first rule and said *re-ven'-ue,* but now we say *rev'-e-nue.*

These two rules will serve as a good general guide to accent. Attention should be paid to the pronunciation of good speakers, and care taken to follow it. In case of doubt the dictionary should be consulted and the proper accent carefully fixed in the mind.

DIVISION OF WORDS

When the words do not fit the line what shall we do? The early printers used only one kind of spaces. In setting a line of type they proceeded until there was no room in the line for the next complete word of the copy. Then they filled out the line with spaces and began the next word on the next line. The length of the register being known in advance and nothing but spaces being used in setting the line, the compositor was spared much that makes composition at once a hard labor and a fine art. The result was an irregular margin at the right such as we now see in typewritten letters.

With improvements in types and typography the squaring out of the page soon came into fashion. In many cases this can be done by the careful use of spaces so as to bring a certain number of words squarely out to the end of the line. There have been printers who have insisted that this should always be done. Their efforts have not, however, been successful. They result in a freakish looking page with white spots in the lines where letters or words have been spaced out to fill the register. It would be better, on the whole, to resort to the practice of the old masters and leave the right-hand margin irregular.

Ordinarily the difficulty has been met by dividing words and putting a part of a word on one line and the rest of it on another, indicating the break by a hyphen. The hyphen in such a case is always the closing character in the [18] first line. Clearly this division must be so made as to assist the reader in his task. The primary purpose of all printing is to be read. Anything that adds to the legibility of the printing improves it; anything that detracts from its legibility harms it. How can we so divide words that the legibility and intelligibility of the text will be maintained, the line justified to register, and the beauty of the page enhanced? These ends — legibility, intelligibility, and beauty — are the aims of all the rules which have been devised for the division of words. These are the things the reader will see and by them he will judge the results. He will probably know nothing about the rules by which the compositor gains his results. The compositor needs to know the rules, but to remember always that they are only means by which to secure results.

There have been several attempts to devise systems of division, but no one of them is thoroughly consistent or universally adopted.

One system requires the division of a word when the pronunciation will permit on the vowel at the end of the syllable. It has the defect of making no provision for syllables that end in consonants. Moreover, if rigorously applied it would give us such divisions as *ca-pa-ci-ty, cata-stro-phe, lexi-co-gra-pher, pre-fe-rence, pro-gno-sti-cate,* and *re-co-gnize.*

Another system requires the division of consolidated words at the junction of their elements, for example:

magn-animous
cata-clysm
found-ation
oceano-graphy
theo-logy
know-ledge
lexi-co-grapher
in-fer-ence
pre-judice
pro-gnos-ticate
pro-position
typo-graphy

In some cases this rule would lead to queer looking divisions. More serious objections are that the system does not provide for words that are long enough to be divided but are yet not consolidated words, and, most of all, that the average compositor is not an accomplished etymologist and knows very little about the derivation, make up, and compounding of the words he has to set up. He may be [19] familiar, for example with the word *rheostat*, but it would puzzle him to tell from what language it is derived, while the word *enclave* would probably send him to the dictionary for meaning as well as derivation, unless he happened to be used to one particular kind of writing.

Another system, and probably on the whole the best one, requires the division of the word on the accented syllable.

theol-ogy
catas-trophe
geog-raphy
lexi-cog-rapher
pref-erence

prog-nos-ticate

It will be noted that some of these examples show division in more than one place, that is on the syllables which bear either the primary or the secondary accent. This rule does not provide for the cases when the division must come on an unaccented syllable. The cases, however, when the division cannot be made to come on either the syllable bearing the primary accent or one bearing a secondary accent will be comparatively few.

RULES FOR DIVISION OF WORDS

I The general rule, then, is to divide according to pronunciation, not according to etymology or any hard and fast rule.

As far as possible, consistently with pronunciation and good spacing, divide according to meaning and derivation, where known.

un-even, not *une-ven*, *auto-mobile*, not *automo-bile*, *en-abled*, not *ena-bled*.

II Divide on a vowel wherever practicable. In case a vowel alone forms a syllable in the middle of a word it should be run into the first line.

busi-ness
sepa-rate
criti-cism
particu-lar
colo-nies
dou-ble
pro-gress
pro-duct
noi-sy
wo-man
pa-tron
me-moir

III When two consonants meet between vowels, and the syllable ends on one consonant, the division may properly [20] be made between the consonants, the pronunciation determining the place of division.

advan-tage
plain-tiff
Wil-liam
exces-sive
scur-rilous
mas-ter
gram-mar
profes-sor
moun-tain

IV When three consonants come together between two vowels the first of which is short, the division comes after the first consonant.

han-dle
chil-dren
frus-trate

V A single consonant between two vowels should be joined to the first vowel, if it is short; if the first vowel is long the consonant goes with the second.

riv-er
ri-val

VI Diphthongs should not be divided.

peo-ple
Cae-sar

VII Words compounded with a prefix should preferably be divided on the prefix.

dis-avow
in-herit
un-concern

VIII The terminations *-able, -ible, -tion, -cial, -tive,* and *-ive* should go over to the next line.

read-able
convert-ible
inten-tion
discuss-ion

The termination *-sion* ordinarily goes over as in

occa-sion
apprehen-sion
cis-sion
declen-sion

Occasionally, however, the strong emphasis needed for the *s* will call for a different arrangement, as in *divis-ion.*

IX The terminations *-ing, -en, -ed, -er, -est,* and the plural *-es* go over to the next line except when the preceding consonant is dou-bled, or when they follow *c* or *g* soft.

lead-ing
beat-en
larg-er, but
lat-ter
for-cing
ran-ging

X Do not end a line with *j* or with *c* or *g* soft.

pro-cess
ne-cessary
pre-judice
prog-eny

XI Adjectives in *ical* divide on the *i.*

physi-cal
inimi-cal

[21] XII In derivatives of words ending in *-t*, the division follows the accent.

objec-tion, not *object-ion*, *defec-tion*, not *defect-ion*, but *respec-tively*, not *respect-ively* and *distinc-tion*, not *distinct-ion*.

XIII Never separate *c* and *g* from the vowels *e*, *i*, and *y* upon which their soft sound depends.

re-li-gion
ca-pa-ci-ty

XIV Never separate *q* from *u*, *qu* is a single sound.

XV Do not divide *nothing*.

XVI Do not divide words of four letters.

XVII Do not divide words of five or six letters if it can be avoided. Good spacing, however, must be considered of first importance.

XVIII In wide measures (20 ems or more) do not divide so as to end or begin a line with a syllable of two letters. Here again, however, good spacing is the first consideration.

XIX Do not divide words of two syllables pronounced as one, including past participles of short words.

heaven
power
prayer
beamed
often

XX Avoid additional hyphens in hyphenated words if possible.

object-lesson
fellow-being
poverty-stricken

XXI Do not separate a divisional mark (*a*), (1) from the matter to which it pertains.

XXII Do not divide an amount stated in figures.

XXIII Do not divide proper names, especially those of persons, if it can be avoided.

XXIV Do not divide initials or such combinations as *a.m.*, *B.C.*

XXV Do not divide the last word on a page so as to carry a part of it to the next page.

XXVI Do not divide the last word of the last full line of a paragraph.

XXVII More than two divisions in successive lines should be avoided.

XXVIII Never divide at all if you can help it.

[22]

IMPORTANCE OF SPACING

It must always be remembered that good spacing is the first consideration. Nothing is more offensive to the eye of a good judge of printing than bad spacing. "Rivers" of white, dark spots, crowded black text, are very serious blemishes to a page. An ordinary book page is a study in color, the colors employed being black and white. Proper combination, balance, and proportion are as important here as in places where a variety of colors is employed. Many of the foregoing rules must be held subject to the exigencies of proper spacing. A rigid adherence, for example, to the rule that not more than two consecutive lines should end with divided words will not justify a badly spaced, unsightly line. There are many things that look worse than a hyphen at the end of the last full line in a paragraph. Avoidance of dividing the last word on a page, however, would justify even bad spacing, because of the gain to the reader. In the last resort, the interests of the reader must always have first consideration.

Division is greatly affected by the length of the measure. A long measure, 18 or 20 ems or more, gives greater opportunity for arranging the spacing, but, on the other hand, makes division on short syllables conspicuous and out of proportion. Very short register, as in two-column Bibles or in cases where illustrations are inserted in the text, presents very great difficulties and often calls for division which would not be allowable elsewhere. Such cases often call for the exercise of the greatest care and ingenuity.

It often happens that the author can be of great assistance to the printer in making a handsome page. A change of a phrase, or even of a word will avoid a difficulty which cannot be avoided by a printer except at the cost of bad division or bad spacing. If the author is a sensible person he will gladly cooperate with the printer in giving his thoughts clothing appropriate to their intrinsic beauty and value. After the printer has exhausted his resources he should not hesitate to carry his troubles to the author.

[23]

DIVISION IN LINES OF DISPLAY

As a rule division is never used in lines of display. In these cases the display is the important thing. Every word long enough to be divided is important enough to be displayed and emphasized. Divided words are weakened words. Lines of irregular lengths are used of set purpose.

In title pages words of bold display must never be divided. In minor lines of display, such as subtitles and summaries, words are often divided. A subheading of two lines should never be divided in the first line when it is possible to turn the full word over on to the next line. The shortening of the first line is never a blemish, but a too short second line following a hyphened first line is always a fault.

There is a school of ultra-artistic composition in book titles which affects a solid squaring up and hesitates at no means to secure its effects. It sets a definite measure and forces the lines into it, dividing words arbitrarily and using no hyphen. This is a passing fancy and will pass as eccentricities always pass. It should not be used unless the author insists upon it. The man who pays the bills has a right to have his work done as he pleases. The intelligent printer, however, will not allow the peculiarities of the individual customer to affect his general practice.

Note

The pupil is referred to the appendix to DeVinne's "Correct Composition" for rules for the division of French, German, and Spanish words. The same appendix contains also a very excellent list of words which are spelled differently by different authorities, together with divisions for them.

[24]

SUPPLEMENTARY READING

Correct Composition. By Theodore L. DeVinne. Oswald Publishing Co., New York.

The Writer's Desk Book. By William Dana Orcutt. Frederick A. Stokes Co., New York.

A Manual for Writers. By John Matthews Manly and John Arthur Powell. The University of Chicago Press, Chicago.

Worcester's New Pronouncing Spelling Book. The American Book Company, New York.

The Art of Writing and Speaking the English Language: Dictionary of Errors. By Sherwin Cody. The Old Greek Press, Chicago.

(This is one of a series of six very excellent but inexpensive little books bearing the same general title and by the same author. They will be found very useful in connection with Part VI of the Typographic Technical Series generally.)

[25]

QUESTIONS

1. Is the spelling of English standardized?

2. How long have we considered correct spelling important?

3. What two causes exist for difficulties in spelling?

4. What are the principal English authorities?

5. What are the principal American authorities?

6. How are these authorities used in printing offices?

7. What are the rights and duties of the author in the matter of spelling?

8. What may be done in matter of "reformed" spelling?

9. What is a safe attitude for the commercial printer toward "reformed" spelling, and why?

10. On what does correct spelling mainly depend?

11. What is the best way to become a good speller?

12. Why is English difficult to pronounce?

13. What is a diphthong?

14. What is a digraph?

15. What are the two sounds each of *c*, *g*, *de*, *th*, and *s*? Give examples of each.

16. How many letters are there in the English alphabet and how many sounds do they express?

17. Upon what does correct pronunciation depend?

18. What is a syllable, and of what does it consist?

19. What peculiar use is made of *l* and *n* in English?

20. How do we treat the parts of a diphthong or digraph?

21. How do we know whether or not these compounds are diphthongs or digraphs?

22. What about vowel combinations?

23. With what should a syllable not end?

24. With what should a syllable not begin?

25. What is the rule regarding prefixes and suffixes?

26. How do we treat two or three consonants capable of beginning a syllable?

[26] 27. How do we treat two or three consonants capable of ending a syllable?

28. How do we treat doubled consonants?

29. What is accent?

30. Do words ever have more than one accent, and why?

31. What are the two general rules for the placing of accent?

32. What did the early printers do when the words did not fit the line, and why?

33. What practice came into use later?

34. What methods of doing this have been devised?

35. What considerations govern practice in this regard?

36. Give two systems of division which have been proposed.

37. What is the general rule for division?

38. What is the rule about vowels?

39. What is the rule about two consonants?

40. What is the rule about three consonants?

41. What should you do with a single consonant between two vowels?

42. How should you treat diphthongs?

43. What is the rule for words compounded with a prefix?

44. What should be done with the terminations -able, -ible, -tion, -cial, -tive, -ive, and -sion?

45. What should be done with the terminations -ing, -en, -ed, -er, and -est, and the plural -es?

46. What letters should not end a line?

47. How are adjectives in *ical* treated?

48. How are derivatives of words ending in -*t* treated?

49. What is the special rule about *c* and *g*?

50. What is the rule about *qu*, and why?

51. What is the rule about *nothing*?

52. What is the rule about words of four letters?

53. How should you treat words of five or six letters?

54. What should be avoided in wide measures?

55. How should you treat words of two syllables pronounced as one?

56. How should hyphenated compounds be treated?

[27] 57. What should you do with divisional marks?

58. How should you treat amounts stated in figures?

59. How should you treat proper names?

60. How are initials and similar combinations treated?

61. What is the rule about the last word on a page?

62. What is the rule about the last word of the last full line of a paragraph?

63. What is the rule about divisions in successive lines?

64. What is the rule about division generally?

65. What effect has spacing on deciding about division?

66. What effect has length of measure on division?

67. What can you do when the text presents unusual difficulty as to spacing and division?

68. What is the rule about division in lines of display, and what is the reason for it?

69. What is the usage with regard to division on title pages?

70. What can you say about eccentricities in the author's or customer's ideas about division and lay-out?

As in the other volumes of this Part, the instructor should not content himself with having the student learn the rules. He should give drills in spelling and pronunciation and should give problems in composition involving the application of rules. Constant and prolonged practice is indispensable to proficiency in all these matters.

[i]

TYPOGRAPHIC TECHNICAL SERIES
FOR APPRENTICES

The following list of publications, comprising the Typographic Technical Series for Apprentices, has been prepared under the supervision of the Committee on Education of the United Typothetae of America for use in trade classes, in course of printing instruction, and by individuals.

Each publication has been compiled by a competent author or group of authors, and carefully edited, the purpose being to provide the printers of the United States—employers, journeymen, and apprentices—with a comprehensive series of handy and inexpensive compendiums of reliable, up-to-date information upon the various branches and specialties of the printing craft, all arranged in orderly fashion for progressive study.

The publications of the series are of uniform size, 5×8 inches. Their general make-up, in typography, illustrations, etc., has been, as far as practicable, kept in harmony throughout. A brief synopsis of the particular contents and other chief features of each volume will be found under each title in the following list.

Each topic is treated in a concise manner, the aim being to embody in each publication as completely as possible all the rudimentary information and essential facts necessary to an understanding of the subject. Care has been taken to make all statements accurate and clear, with the purpose of bringing essential information within the understanding of beginners in the different fields of study. Wherever practicable, simple and well-defined drawings and illustrations have been used to assist in giving additional clearness to the text.

In order that the pamphlets may be of the greatest possible help for use in trade-school classes and for self-instruction, each title is accompanied by a list of Review Questions covering essential items of the subject matter. A short Glossary of technical terms belonging to the subject or department treated is also added to many of the books.

These are the Official Text-books of the United Typothetae of America.

Address all orders and inquiries to Committee on Education, United Typothetae of America, Chicago, Illinois, U.S.A.

[ii]

PART I—*Types, Tools, Machines, and Materials*

- **1. Type: a Primer of Information By A.A. Stewart**

Relating to the mechanical features of printing types; their sizes, font schemes, etc., with a brief description of their manufacture. 44 pp.; illustrated; 74 review questions; glossary.

- **2. Compositors' Tools and Materials By A.A. Stewart**

A primer of information about composing sticks, galleys, leads, brass rules, cutting and mitering machines, etc. 47 pp.; illustrated; 50 review questions; glossary.

- **3. Type Cases, Composing Room Furniture By A.A. Stewart**

A primer of information about type cases, work stands, cabinets, case racks, galley racks, standing galleys, etc. 43 pp.; illustrated; 33 review questions; glossary.

- **4. Imposing Tables and Lock-up Appliances By A.A. Stewart**

Describing the tools and materials used in locking up forms for the press, including some modern utilities for special purposes. 59 pp.; illustrated; 70 review questions; glossary.

- **5. Proof Presses By A.A. Stewart**

A primer of information about the customary methods and machines for taking printers' proofs. 40 pp.; illustrated; 41 review questions; glossary.

- **6. Platen Printing Presses By Daniel Baker**

A primer of information regarding the history and mechanical construction of platen printing presses, from the original hand press to the modern job press, to which is added a chapter on automatic presses of small size. 51 pp.; illustrated; 49 review questions; glossary.

- **7. Cylinder Printing Presses By Herbert L. Baker**

Being a study of the mechanism and operation of the principal types of cylinder printing machines. 64 pp.; illustrated; 47 review questions; glossary.

- **8. Mechanical Feeders and Folders By William E. Spurrier**

The history and operation of modern feeding and folding machines; with hints on their care and adjustments. Illustrated; review questions; glossary.

- **9. Power for Machinery in Printing Houses By Carl F. Scott**

A treatise on the methods of applying power to printing presses and allied machinery with particular reference to electric drive. 53 pp.; illustrated; 69 review questions; glossary.

- **10. Paper Cutting Machines By Niel Gray, Jr.**

A primer of information about paper and card trimmers, hand-lever cutters, power cutters, and other automatic machines for cutting paper, 70 pp.; illustrated; 115 review questions; glossary.

- **11. Printers' Rollers By A.A. Stewart**

A primer of information about the composition, manufacture, and care of inking rollers. 46 pp.; illustrated; 61 review questions; glossary.

- **12. Printing Inks By Philip Ruxton**

Their composition, properties and manufacture (reprinted by permission from Circular No. 53, United States Bureau of Standards); together with some helpful suggestions about the everyday use of printing inks by Philip Ruxton. 80 pp.; 100 review questions; glossary.

[iii]

• **13. How Paper is Made By William Bond Wheelwright**

A primer of information about the materials and processes of manufacturing paper for printing and writing. 68 pp.; illustrated; 62 review questions; glossary.

• **14. Relief Engravings By Joseph P. Donovan**

Brief history and non-technical description of modern methods of engraving; woodcut, zinc plate, halftone; kind of copy for reproduction; things to remember when ordering engravings. Illustrated; review questions; glossary.

• **15. Electrotyping and Stereotyping By Harris B. Hatch and A.A. Stewart**

A primer of information about the processes of electrotyping and stereotyping. 94 pp.; illustrated; 129 review questions; glossaries.

PART II — *Hand and Machine Composition*

• **16. Typesetting By A.A. Stewart**

A handbook for beginners, giving information about justifying, spacing, correcting, and other matters relating to typesetting. Illustrated; review questions; glossary.

• **17. Printers' Proofs By A.A. Stewart**

The methods by which they are made, marked, and corrected, with observations on proofreading. Illustrated; review questions; glossary.

56

- **18. First Steps in Job Composition By Camille DeVéze**

Suggestions for the apprentice compositor in getting his first jobs, especially about the important little things which go to make good display in typography. 63 pp.; examples; 55 review questions; glossary.

- **19. General Job Composition**

How the job compositor handles business stationery, programs and miscellaneous work. Illustrated; review questions; glossary.

- **20. Book Composition By J.W. Bothwell**

Chapters from DeVinne's "Modern Methods of Book Composition," revised and arranged for this series of text-books by J.W. Bothwell of The DeVinne Press, New York. Part I: Composition of pages. Part II: Imposition of pages. 229 pp.; illustrated; 525 review questions; glossary.

- **21. Tabular Composition By Robert Seaver**

A study of the elementary forms of table composition, with examples of more difficult composition. 36 pp.; examples; 45 review questions.

- **22. Applied Arithmetic By E.E. Sheldon**

Elementary arithmetic applied to problems of the printing trade, calculation of materials, paper weights and sizes, with standard tables and rules for computation, each subject amplified with examples and exercises. 159 pp.

- **23. Typecasting and Composing Machines A.W. Finlay, Editor**

Section I — The Linotype **By L.A. Hornstein**
Section II — The Monotype **By Joseph Hays**
Section III — The Intertype **By Henry W. Cozzens**

Section IV—Other Typecasting and Typesetting Machines
By Frank H. Smith

A brief history of typesetting machines, with descriptions of their mechanical principles and operations. Illustrated; review questions; glossary.

PART III—*Imposition and Stonework* [iv]

- **24. Locking Forms for the Job Press By Frank S. Henry**

Things the apprentice should know about locking up small forms, and about general work on the stone. Illustrated; review questions; glossary.

- **25. Preparing Forms for the Cylinder Press By Frank S. Henry**

Pamphlet and catalog imposition; margins; fold marks, etc. Methods of handling type forms and electrotype forms. Illustrated; review questions; glossary.

PART IV—*Presswork*

- **26. Making Ready on Platen Presses By T.G. McGrew**

The essential parts of a press and their functions; distinctive features of commonly used machines. Preparing the tympan, regulating the impression, underlaying and overlaying, setting gauges, and other details explained. Illustrated; review questions; glossary.

- **27. Cylinder Presswork By T.G. McGrew**

Preparing the press; adjustment of bed and cylinder, form rollers, ink fountain, grippers and delivery systems. Underlaying and overlaying; modern overlay methods. Illustrated; review questions; glossary.

- **28. Pressroom Hints and Helps By Charles L. Dunton**

Describing some practical methods of pressroom work, with directions and useful information relating to a variety of printing-press problems. 87 pp.; 176 review questions.

• 29. Reproductive Processes of the Graphic Arts By A.W. Elson

A primer of information about the distinctive features of the relief, the intaglio, and the planographic processes of printing. 84 pp.; illustrated; 100 review questions; glossary.

PART V — *Pamphlet and Book Binding*

• 30. Pamphlet Binding By Bancroft L. Goodwin

A primer of information about the various operations employed in binding pamphlets and other work in the bindery. Illustrated; review questions; glossary.

• 31. Book Binding By John J. Pleger

Practical information about the usual operations in binding books; folding; gathering, collating, sewing, forwarding, finishing. Case making and cased-in books. Hand work and machine work. Job and blank-book binding. Illustrated; review questions; glossary.

PART VI — *Correct Literary Composition*

• 32. Word Study and English Grammar By F.W. Hamilton

A primer of information about words, their relations, and their uses. 68 pp.; 84 review questions; glossary.

• 33. Punctuation By F.W. Hamilton

A primer of information about the marks of punctuation and their use, both grammatically and typographically. 56 pp.; 59 review questions; glossary.

[v]

• 34. Capitals By F.W. Hamilton

A primer of information about capitalization, with some practical typographic hints as to the use of capitals. 48 pp.; 92 review questions; glossary.

- ### 35. Division of Words **By F.W. Hamilton**

Rules for the division of words at the ends of lines, with remarks on spelling, syllabication and pronunciation. 42 pp.; 70 review questions.

- ### 36. Compound Words **By F.W. Hamilton**

A study of the principles of compounding, the components of compounds, and the use of the hyphen. 34 pp.; 62 review questions.

- ### 37. Abbreviations and Signs **By F.W. Hamilton**

A primer of information about abbreviations and signs, with classified lists of those in most common use. 58 pp.; 32 review questions.

- ### 38. The Uses of Italic **By F.W. Hamilton**

A primer of information about the history and uses of italic letters. 31 pp.; 37 review questions.

- ### 39. Proofreading **By Arnold Levitas**

The technical phases of the proofreader's work; reading, marking, revising, etc.; methods of handling proofs and copy. Illustrated by examples. 59 pp.; 69 review questions; glossary.

- ### 40. Preparation of Printers' Copy **By F.W. Hamilton**

Suggestions for authors, editors, and all who are engaged in preparing copy for the composing room. 36 pp.; 67 review questions.

- ### 41. Printers' Manual of Style

A reference compilation of approved rules, usages, and suggestions relating to uniformity in punctuation, capitalization, abbreviations, numerals, and kindred features of composition.

• 42. The Printer's Dictionary By A.A. Stewart

A handbook of definitions and miscellaneous information about various processes of printing, alphabetically arranged. Technical terms explained. Illustrated.

PART VII—*Design, Color, and Lettering*

• 43. Applied Design for Printers By Harry L. Gage

A handbook of the principles of arrangement, with brief comment on the periods of design which have most influenced printing. Treats of harmony, balance, proportion, and rhythm; motion; symmetry and variety; ornament, esthetic and symbolic. 37 illustrations; 46 review questions; glossary; bibliography.

• 44. Elements of Typographic Design By Harry L. Gage

Applications of the principles of decorative design. Building material of typography paper, types, ink, decorations and illustrations. Handling of shapes. Design of complete book, treating each part. Design of commercial forms and single units. Illustrations; review questions, glossary; bibliography.

[vi]

• 45. Rudiments of Color in Printing By Harry L. Gage

Use of color: for decoration of black and white, for broad poster effect, in combinations of two, three, or more printings with process engravings. Scientific nature of color, physical and chemical. Terms in which color may be discussed: hue, value, intensity. Diagrams in color, scales and combinations. Color theory of process engraving. Experiments with color. Illustrations in full color, and on various papers. Review questions; glossary; bibliography.

• 46. Lettering in Typography By Harry L. Gage

Printer's use of lettering: adaptability and decorative effect. Development of historic writing and lettering and its influence on type design. Classification of general forms in lettering. Application of design to lettering. Drawing for reproduction. Fully illustrated; review questions; glossary; bibliography.

• 47. Typographic Design in Advertising By Harry L. Gage

The printer's function in advertising. Precepts upon which advertising is based. Printer's analysis of his copy. Emphasis, legibility, attention, color. Method of studying advertising typography. Illustrations; review questions; glossary; bibliography.

• 48. Making Dummies and Layouts By Harry L. Gage

A layout: the architectural plan. A dummy: the imitation of a proposed final effect. Use of dummy in sales work. Use of layout. Function of layout man. Binding schemes for dummies. Dummy envelopes. Illustrations; review questions; glossary; bibliography.

PART VIII — *History of Printing*

• 49. Books Before Typography By F.W. Hamilton

A primer of information about the invention of the alphabet and the history of bookmaking up to the invention of movable types. 62 pp.; illustrated; 64 review questions.

- 50. **The Invention of Typography** By F.W. Hamilton

A brief sketch of the invention of printing and how it came about. 64 pp.; 62 review questions.

- 51. **History of Printing—Part I** By F.W. Hamilton

A primer of information about the beginnings of printing, the development of the book, the development of printers' materials, and the work of the great pioneers. 63 pp.; 55 review questions.

- 52. **History of Printing—Part II** By F.W. Hamilton

A brief sketch of the economic conditions of the printing industry from 1450 to 1789, including government regulations, censorship, internal conditions and industrial relations. 94 pp.; 128 review questions.

- 53. **Printing in England** By F.W. Hamilton

A short history of printing in England from Caxton to the present time. 89 pp.; 65 review questions.

- 54. **Printing in America** By F.W. Hamilton

A brief sketch of the development of the newspaper, and some notes on publishers who have especially contributed to printing. 98 pp.; 84 review questions.

- 55. **Type and Presses in America** By F.W. Hamilton

A brief historical sketch of the development of type casting and press building in the United States. 52 pp.; 61 review questions.

[vii] PART IX—*Cost Finding and Accounting*

- 56. **Elements of Cost in Printing** By Henry P. Porter

Hygiene in the printing trade; a study of conditions old and new; practical suggestions for improvement; protective appliances and rules for safety.

- **63. Topical Index By F.W. Hamilton**

A book of reference covering the topics treated in the Typographic Technical Series, alphabetically arranged.

- **64. Courses of Study By F.W. Hamilton**

A guidebook for teachers, with outlines and suggestions for classroom and shop work.

[viii]

ACKNOWLEDGMENT

This series of Typographic Text-books is the result of the splendid co-operation of a large number of firms and individuals engaged in the printing business and its allied industries in the United States of America.

The Committee on Education of the United Typothetae of America, under whose auspices the books have been prepared and published, acknowledges its indebtedness for the generous assistance rendered by the many authors, printers, and others identified with this work.

While due acknowledgment is made on the title and copyright pages of those contributing to each book, the Committee nevertheless felt that a group list of co-operating firms would be of interest.

The following list is not complete, as it includes only those who have co-operated in the production of a portion of the volumes, constituting the first printing. As soon as the entire list of books comprising the Typographic Technical Series has been completed (which the Committee hopes will be at an early date), the full list will be printed in each volume.

The Committee also desires to acknowledge its indebtedness to the many subscribers to this Series who have patiently awaited its publication.

Committee on Education,
United Typothetae of America.
Henry P. Porter, *Chairman,*
E. Lawrence Fell,
A.M. Glossbrenner,
J. Clyde Oswald,
Toby Rubovits.

Frederick W. Hamilton, *Education Director.*

[ix]

CONTRIBUTORS

For Composition and Electrotypes

Isaac H. Blanchard Company, New York, N.Y.
S.H. Burbank & Co., Philadelphia, Pa.
J.S. Cushing & Co., Norwood, Mass.
The DeVinne Press, New York, N.Y.
R.R. Donnelley & Sons Co., Chicago, Ill.
Geo. H. Ellis Co., Boston, Mass.
Evans-Winter-Hebb, Detroit, Mich.
Franklin Printing Company, Philadelphia, Pa.
F.H. Gilson Company, Boston, Mass.
Stephen Greene & Co., Philadelphia, Pa.
W.F. Hall Printing Co., Chicago, Ill.
J.B. Lippincott Co., Philadelphia, Pa.
McCalla & Co. Inc., Philadelphia, Pa.
The Patteson Press, New York, New York
The Plimpton Press, Norwood, Mass.
Poole Bros., Chicago, Ill.
Edward Stern & Co., Philadelphia, Pa.
The Stone Printing & Mfg. Co., Roanoke, Va.
C.D. Traphagen, Lincoln, Neb.
The University Press, Cambridge, Mass.

For Composition

Boston Typothetae School of Printing, Boston, Mass.
William F. Fell Co., Philadelphia, Pa.
The Kalkhoff Company, New York, N.Y.
Oxford-Print, Boston, Mass.
Toby Rubovits, Chicago, Ill.

For Electrotypes

Blomgren Brothers Co., Chicago, Ill.
Flower Steel Electrotyping Co., New York, N.Y.
C.J. Peters & Son Co., Boston, Mass.
Royal Electrotype Co., Philadelphia, Pa.

H.C. Whitcomb & Co., Boston, Mass.

For Engravings

American Type Founders Co., Boston, Mass.
C.B. Cottrell & Sons Co., Westerly, R.I.
Golding Manufacturing Co., Franklin, Mass.
Harvard University, Cambridge, Mass.
Inland Printer Co., Chicago, Ill.
Lanston Monotype Machine Company, Philadelphia, Pa.
Mergenthaler Linotype Company, New York, N.Y.
Geo. H. Morrill Co., Norwood, Mass.
Oswald Publishing Co., New York, N.Y.
The Printing Art, Cambridge, Mass.
B.D. Rising Paper Company, Housatonic, Mass.
The Vandercook Press, Chicago, Ill.

For Book Paper

American Writing Paper Co., Holyoke, Mass.
West Virginia Pulp & Paper Co., Mechanicville, N.Y.